Bibliografische Information der Deutschen Nationalbibliothek:

Die Deutsche Bibliothek verzeichnet diese Publikation in der Deutschen National-bibliografie; detaillierte bibliografische Daten sind im Internet über http://dnb.d-nb.de/ abrufbar.

Impressum:

Copyright © 2018 GRIN Verlag
Druck und Bindung: Books on Demand GmbH, Norderstedt Germany
ISBN: 9783668812727

Dieses Buch bei GRIN:

https://www.grin.com/document/442324

Atul Apte

Significance of semantically complete terminologies in unsupervised (self) learning

GRIN Verlag

GRIN - Your knowledge has value

Der GRIN Verlag publiziert seit 1998 wissenschaftliche Arbeiten von Studenten, Hochschullehrern und anderen Akademikern als eBook und gedrucktes Buch. Die Verlagswebsite www.grin.com ist die ideale Plattform zur Veröffentlichung von Hausarbeiten, Abschlussarbeiten, wissenschaftlichen Aufsätzen, Dissertationen und Fachbüchern.

Besuchen Sie uns im Internet:

http://www.grin.com/

http://www.facebook.com/grincom

http://www.twitter.com/grin_com

Significance of semantically complete terminologies in unsupervised (self) learning

A case study of emerging terminology for blockchain technology

Atul Apte

Introduction

The notion of semantically complete terminology came to my mind in context of self-learning. Particularly when learning a new technology like blockchain. Most people who are actively learning about blockchain also are interested in understanding the true and complete meaning of blockchain. This paper explores the characteristics of semantically complete terminology for blockchain and its significance to self-learning and in accelerating the learning process.

The first step in learning blockchain, is asking the question – what is blockchain? In response, we typically get different answers; including many variations of an answer thereby causing confusion rather than clarity. One common factor in every answer is the use of _blockchain_ as a technical term followed by an explanation of the term's meaning. For e.g., in some answers the term blockchain is explained as a particular software architecture or design pattern. In other answers blockchain explanations center on a particular type of technology platform or product (e.g. Hyperledger, Corda, Ethereum, etc...). Some answers use the term blockchain to represent a particular type of outcome (e.g. distributed ledger). Interestingly enough, some answers also tend to include a series of statements or additional explanations about what blockchain is _not_ (e.g. blockchain is _not_ a database). This type of semantic contradictions can slow down self-learning, although in the end we may indeed learn and understand blockchain correctly (provided we persist with the learning).

This raises a more fundamental question about the creation or selection of technical terms and their critical role in forming a semantically complete terminology (a set of complimentary technical terms) for a subject matter. We will explore this question further in the context of learning blockchain technology.

In the context of self-learning a subject matter (e.g. technology), individual technical terms matter because each term triggers a different, initial perception in our minds. These initial perceptions prompt us to form immediate opinions that can be technically right or wrong and indeed difficult to overcome. To promote proper grasping and easier learning of new technologies, we need a terminology that represents a subject matter holistically from a semantic perspective. It is not a question about less ambiguous and more precise technical terms, but semantically appropriate (representative) terms.

The objective of this paper is not to criticize or judge any particular technical term, but to ensure we have the right set of technical terms to appropriately represent blockchain technology. It is assumed that this would enable easier and accurate understanding (learning). To verify this, we will explore some of the commonly used technical terms associated with blockchain technology (e.g. blockchain, distributed ledger technology, shared ledgers) and determine if they represent the holistic intent, mechanisms, and consequences (positive and negative) of blockchain technology. We will then consider adding some new technical terms with the intent of strengthening blockchain terminology and facilitating better learning and quicker understanding of blockchain technology in its entirety.

If this approach proves to be effective, we could apply it to learning other emerging technologies in future.

Fundamental steps in (self) learning a subject matter

When we start to learn a new subject matter like a new technology or a new technical topic, our initial perceptions are very important. Typically, we get acquainted with a new technology or topic through some form of technical terms (e.g. blockchain). This acquaintance is the first step in our learning process and hence very significant. We may form some very accurate perception of the subject matter or we may form some incorrect perceptions that could lead to wrong opinions and make learning difficult. It is also possible that the acquaintance created by technical terms does not have any impact on our learning.

For example, when learning about blockchain, we will certainly encounter these three terms – blockchain, distributed ledger technology, and shared ledger. Are all or any of these terms entirely representative of the subject matter? Do these terms help us learn blockchain technology or could these terms create some incorrect perceptions that we need to overcome through deeper dives into understanding blockchain technology?

We need to take the issue of semantic completeness in terminologies seriously. Gathering all the technical terms associated with a subject matter is not a simple task as individual technical terms are often created in different contexts and at different times. For example the creators of a new technology may define some technical terms to <u>represent</u> and <u>communicate</u> the invented technology with their peers and like-minded people. Similarly, marketing of the new technology could lead to some other technical terms intended to <u>differentiate</u> the invented technology. Industry analysts may create some more technical terms to put the invented technology in a <u>broader</u> technical or non-technical context.

So, the actual terminology becomes a concoction of terms. Generally speaking, when learning a technology or a technical subject, we need to discover and understand the meanings in three different dimensions – conceptual, logical, and physical. It is very difficult to define or find <u>one</u> technical term that can trigger initial perceptions that can lead to an understanding of the multi-dimensional meanings.

So the first step in learning a (technical) subject matter should be to assess the semantic quality of the terminology and its individual technical terms. The goal is to prevent any misconceptions or misleading perceptions, which could hinder our learning. The quality of a terminology is determined by its semantic completeness, which depends on the set of semantically representative terms. If we detect any gaps in the semantic quality of a terminology, we can make the necessary effort to create and propose additional semantically representative terms to establish the necessary semantic completeness.

To assess semantic quality of a terminology, we need a criteria that is applicable at a granular level – individual technical terms and at a holistic level - a collection of technical terms. The basic premise for assessing the quality is to ensure we have an appropriate set of technical terms that would actually facilitate learning. Before we spend any time in assessing a term, it is important that we understand the significance of semantically complete terminology in creating an easier, quicker, and ultimately more efficient learning path.

When one decides to learn a subject matter like blockchain technology on their own, figuring out an appropriate starting point can be a challenge. Other than scanning the web for documents (there is no shortage of documents) or downloading an open source stack and coding a blockchain app, there is not much in terms of a recommended approach for self-learning blockchain. Multiple technical terms like blockchain, shared ledgers, distributed ledger technology can only confuse the learning process.

Most of us will agree that our learning is complete when we know what a subject matter is and what it isn't. Let's also assume that initial perceptions of a subject matter are essential to learning. In fact, we may not be consciously aware of the perceptions formed in our minds when we get acquainted with terms. For example, we could form an initial perception of mathematics as a being difficult subject matter when we become acquainted with (abstract) mathematical terms.

Tenative model of the role of terminology in learning a subject matter

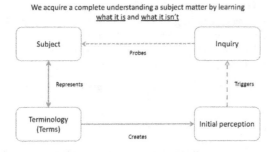

We acquire a complete understanding a subject matter by learning what it is and what it isn't

Can a single term represent the essence of a subject matter?
Could a set of disjointed terms represent a subject matter holistically?

Why should we look for semantic completeness in terminology?

1. We need to start our learning of a subject matter with broader (initial) perceptions

2. We need comprehensive inquiry to probe into a subject matter

3. We need to accelerate understanding and while avoiding any misunderstandings by validating or invalidating our initial perceptions of the subject matter

But maybe things could be different if we have semantically representative terms for a subject matter. Initial perceptions created by such terms could actually trigger inquiries that help us probe into the subject matter. The purpose of probing is to validate or invalidate our initial perceptions, leading to a holistic (what it is and what it isn't) understanding of the subject matter. But, is every semantically representative term useful in such learning? For e.g. the iconic term $E = mc^2$ may be representative of the underlying physics theory, but can it accelerate the learning?

Can there be one semantically representative term for an entire subject matter? Or, do we need multiple semantically representative terms to represent all parts of a subject matter? To figure this out, we need to explore the characteristic of semantically representative technical terms and the making of a semantically complete terminology.

A semantically complete terminology (terms) has the capability to create appropriate initial perceptions that can trigger a comprehensive inquiry into probing (exploring) the associated subject matter. Without an initial perception, self-learning becomes an unproductive cycle of asking questions and being unsatisfied with answers.

What do we mean by semantically complete technical terminology? In the context of learning, semantic completeness is not necessarily a linguistic feature (although the choice of words can have a big impact on our initial perceptions and ultimate understanding). Semantic completeness is about being representative of an associated subject matter.

A term becomes representative when there is a relationship between a term and some part(s) of a subject matter. This relationship is not just a mnemonic but an abbreviated statement. The challenge is that the abbreviations can be any combination of ambiguous or precise, abstract or concrete. A technical term that is unambiguous (specific) and is related to an abstract or concrete part of a subject matter, tends to be more effective in helping us learn.

We obviously cannot expect a single technical term to completely represent an entire subject matter. Therefore, a semantically complete terminology is a collection of a semantically representative terms. There is no pre-determined sweet-spot for the number of terms necessary to form a semantically complete terminology.

Tentative model for defining a semantically complete technical terminology

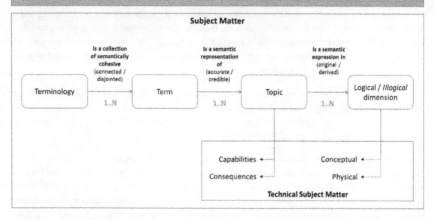

It seems that the key to semantically representative terms is the relationship of the term with a specific "topic" of the subject matter.

For technical terms, there are two types of topics – capabilities and consequences that are more significant from a semantic completeness perspective. A technical term that represents any combination of capabilities and/or consequences becomes semantically representative and contributes to the semantic completion of a terminology. This notion is particularly applicable to technology, where our desire or objective centers on understanding the capabilities and the consequences of using the technology.

There is a further attribute to representative technical terms. It is about the logical dimensions of technical meaning, which shapes our understanding of the subject matter. There are two logical dimensions that are particularly significant for technical subject matters – conceptual and physical dimensions. Individual, semantically representative technical terms should represent a topic (combinations of capabilities and consequences) through abbreviated expressions in one or both logical dimensions.

Does this mean that a terminology is not semantically complete unless there are terms to represent the meaning of all topics of a subject matter across both logical dimensions? This makes sense because learning a technical subject matter means we attain complete (full and holistic) understanding of all its topics across conceptual and physical dimensions. Any learning that occurs in only one logical dimension results in partial understanding of the subject matter.

It is highly unlikely that we can define or compile a semantically complete terminology. Particularly for emerging technologies (e.g. blockchain), a more realistic scenario is that the terminology begins with a concoction of terms and evolves into a semantically complete terminology. This can happen by applying and improving the terminology through feedback and analysis of self-learning outcomes.

For technical a subject matter, semantically representative terms create two kinds of initial perceptions – an initial perception of what the technology "is" or an initial perception of what the technology "isn't". So, it would be logical to think that a semantically complete terminology that creates a complete, initial perception of "what is" provides a direct path for learning. Correspondingly, a semantically complete terminology that create a complete, initial perception of "what isn't" provides an indirect path for learning. This logic is based on the assumption that "what is" is narrower domain compared with the "what isn't", which tends to be a much broader domain.

We could consider the "what is" terminology as the "fundamental" terminology of a subject matter and the "what isn't" terminology as a "reinforcing" terminology. Common sense may tell us that a fundamental terminology would be relatively smaller (finite terms) than its corresponding reinforcing terminology which could be very big (infinite terms).

Any terminology that is neither entirely fundamental nor reinforcing may become ineffective for learning. This is indeed a binary position about which type of terminology is effective and which is ineffective. However, we won't ponder if this position is right or wrong, and simply move forward with further exploration of this position in the context of an actual case study. Blockchain technology is an ideal subject for a case study as it's an emerging technology, many people are actively learning the technology and certain terms are highly prevalent. This means we can putting the idea of semantically complete terminology to test with blockchain technology could prove useful.

The "quality" of a terminology is about its effectiveness in facilitating the holistic learning and understanding of a subject matter. It is not about identifying and removing any semantic or linguistic defects in the terminology. Although, it is possible that in ensuring the effectiveness of a terminology, any inherent semantic defects will be removed.

An effective terminology has two qualities - a semantically complete set (collection) of semantically representative terms for all the topics of a subject matter. The first quality being that it is a collection of terms (exception being when a single term is sufficient). The second quality being each term in the collection is semantically representative of one or more topics. These qualities apply consistently to any type of terminology (foundation and reinforcing terminologies).

Is it possible to ascertain the quality (effectiveness) of a terminology especially when two or more terminologies may have semantic differences combined with linguistic similarities? Maybe we can simplify how we determine the quality of a terminology by considering its contextual use (e.g. self-learning). This means, that we may find a specific terminology is semantically complete for self-learning but not necessarily for other purpose or context.

In the context of self-learning, we may be able to determine the quality of terminologies by leveraging the tentative models for self-learning and semantically complete terms. This implies that we track the initial perceptions, inquiries, and the resulting understandings from each term of a terminology. If the results (understanding) prove to be correct (accurate or credible) then the terminology is effective.

Steps for assessing the semantic quality of a foundational or reinforcing terminology:

- Step 1: capture and share the initial perceptions that emerge in our minds by reading or stating a specific technical term
- Step 2: capture and share the types of inquiries we decide to use in probing the subject matter represented by the technical term
- Step 3: capture and share any validations or invalidations of each initial perception
- Step 4: compare the shared validations and invalidations of each initial perception
- Step 5: after repeating steps 1 – 4 for each term of the terminology, determine any gaps (unrepresented topics, and unexpressed logical dimensions)
- Step 6: propose additional terms and repeat steps 1 – 5 until there are no gaps
- Step 7: publish the semantically complete terminology

As part of testing the quality of a technical terminology, we need to establish some basic understanding of the semantic origins of each term. Knowing the origins of a technical term is useful in determining the potential risk of associated overloaded meanings. Most technical terms are either "crafted" to represent a particular topic of a subject matter or emerge in a colloquial settings, through conversations about the subject matter.

The semantic completeness test will result in a classification of terms as either colloquial terms or designer terms. The important factor in this classification will be the determination of any overloaded meanings. This can help in preventing designer terms from morphing into colloquial terms and in maintaining the quality of a terminology.

Why is this classification of terms important to testing the quality of a terminology? If the composition of a terminology has a greater % of colloquial terms, then there is greater risk or probability of the terminology not being conducive for efficient self-learning. It is indeed natural that over time and with frequent use, designer terms can become colloquial terms. This means we may need to create (craft) new designer terms to maintain a terminology.

Classifcation of technical terms

Class of technical terms	Foundational terminology	Reinforcing terminology	Risk of overloaded terms
Colloquial terms	> 25%	> 50%	High
Designer terms	> 75 %	> 50 %	Low

Classifcation of blockchain technical terms

Class of technical terms	Blockchain foundational terminology
Colloquial (current) terms	1. Blockchain 2. Distributed ledger technology 3. Smart contract
Designer (hypothetical) terms	1. Subsystem for recording transactions 2. Decentralized generation of immutable data chains 3. Replicated system of record

The terminology for blockchain technology maybe a long list of terms but we can conduct a semantic completeness tests on some of the popular (colloquial) terms like – blockchain, distributed ledger technology, and smart contract. We can extend this test by considering the addition of three "designer" technical terms to figure out if adding new terms can deliver a semantically complete terminology. The tests will stick with the assumption that not every technical term will prove to be effective and efficient for self-learning.

Blockchain is a unique term because not only is it new, but it's also the subject matter. So, irrespective of its effectiveness in self-learning, it will always be part of the terminology for blockchain technology.

Likely initial perceptions:

Blockchain is a new word and hence there is little to no risk of the term having any overloaded meanings. In fact, the term has some mysterious undertones as there are no previous learning that become automatically applicable either. So the likely initial perceptions will be about the intrigue associated with blockchain technology. The "chain" part of the term blockchain is likely to create perceptions of links between blocks. In fact there is ample evidence of this in visual diagrams created to explain blockchain technology.

The perception that the term "blockchain" represents the essence of blockchain technology may arise. Although, it's possible that this initial perceptions may include uncertainty about what type of topics (capabilities and consequences) are associated with blockchain technology.

So, do these initial perceptions have any value in terms of self-learning? That depends on what type of inquiries into blockchain technology take place as a result of these perceptions. The apparent vagueness of the term "blockchain" drives us to explore the subject matter further, which is a good thing. Also, as an unloaded term the exploration of blockchain technology can happen without any correct or incorrect presumptions.

Likely inquiries triggered by initial perceptions:

The initial perceptions certainly trigger the basic inquiry – what is blockchain technology? This is a broad, open-ended inquiry and as such can lead to any number of different paths for probing the subject matter. There is a possibility that the exploration can be misguided by the many definitions and descriptions that intend to explain blockchain technology.

If the inquiry centers on the technical topics, then the subsequent probing is likely to be narrow and productive. A more pertinent inquiry could be one of the following, is blockchain a technical capability, is blockhain a technical consequence, or is blockchain a technical capability and consequence.

If the probability of the broader, open-ended inquiry occurring is higher than the narrower probing of capabilities and consequences, then the term blockchain is not an efficient term for self-learning. To some extent the answer as to which type of inquiry (broader or narrower) is likely to occur depends on the learning process. If someone is starting the learning process then the broader inquiry is most likely to occur. But, if we encounter the term blockchain while learning some other technical subject matter, then the probability of a pertinent inquiry occurring could be much higher.

In short, new terms like blockchain do raise our curiosity but its effectiveness in self-learning needs careful determination.

There is a growing trend to classify blockchain technology as distributed ledger technology. This could be an attempt to create a unifying technical term to represent variations of blockchain. But unlike the term blockchain, every word of the term "distributed ledger technology" is not only familiar but is overloaded with meanings. Hence, assessing the effectiveness of this term to self-learning is highly significant.

Likely initial perceptions:

Familiar words and overloaded meaning raises the risk of presumptive misunderstandings. The word distributed has very specific dynamics in technology and computerized systems. So, it shouldn't be surprising if perceptions that draw from previous understandings of other subject matters like distributed computing, distributed processing, or distributed databases get triggered. But are such perceptions valid? If yes, to what extent are the similarities between blockchain technology and other distributed technologies? If blockchain technology is not distributed in the sense of other distributed technologies, is including this word (distributed) in a blockchain term correct?

Certainly the word "ledger" is also capable of triggering an initial perception. Anyone with a background in accounting is likely to perceive some similarities with the concept of ledger and ledger keeping. Conceptual perceptions can be holistic and surprisingly accurate or highly misleading. Certainly, a thorough inquiry and probing of blockchain technology is necessary to uncover if associating the term ledger to blockchain is indeed valid.

At the same time, the word "technology" can create perceptions of tangible artifacts in the physical dimension. Does this clarify or complicate the overall term? Either way an inquiry into how the conceptual ledger connects with the physical technology is required.

Likely inquiries triggered by initial perceptions:

The term "distributed ledger technology" is a mixture of conceptual, physical, and other subject matters. This makes it a complex term (much more complex than the term blockchain). Is distributed ledger technology a different subject matter? This is a critical inquiry. If true, is blockchain technology a type of distributed ledger technology? If this is also true, blockchain technology is constrained by the attributes, properties, and other factors of distributed ledger technology. Are all topics of distributed ledger technology applicable to blockchain technology?

In short, this seems like a classic example of an indirect learning path as we may indeed explore the distributed ledger technology subject matter prior to or at the same time as exploring the blockchain technology subject matter.

It is hard to tell whether the introduction of "distributed ledger technology" actually helps or hurts self-learning of blockchain technology. It may be better to defer the use of terms that draw on similarities with other subject matter until after a correct understanding of the subject matter (blockchain) is established.

Exotic terms tend to create skeptical perceptions that frequently lead to misrepresentation of the subject matters actual capabilities and consequences. Smart contract is indeed an exotic term. As an exotic and colloquial term, it can easily accumulate overloaded meanings and propagate misrepresentations.

Likely initial perceptions:

Individually, both the terms contract and smart are familiar. "Contract" has immediate familiarity in the physical dimension and the term "smart" is mostly familiar in the conceptual dimension. However, the combined term – "Smart contract" is likely to create initial perceptions that are highly skeptical of this semantic association.

Negative perceptions can become a hurdle for learning a subject matter. In fact, if a terminology ends up triggering a large number of negative perceptions, learning that subject matter can become very difficult. It is better for a foundational terminology not to have any terms that can lead to skeptical perceptions.

However, when properly channeled, skepticism and doubt can be an excellent trigger for learning. But this requires supervision or guidance. In a self-learning scenario, appropriate channeling of skepticism is difficult to achieve. The important thing is to balance the initial skepticism with the possibility of the term being representative and let subsequent inquiries into the blockchain subject matter validate or invalidate the term "smart contract".

Likely inquiries triggered by initial perceptions:

Inquiries triggered by skeptical perceptions are likely to center on validating the initial doubt (confirming the initial negative perception). Questions like what makes a blockchain contract "smart" will arise. This can easily lead to inquiries into adjacent subject matters like what is the meaning of "smart"? Distractions from learning the actual subject matter (blockchain) is very likely.

Will the initial skeptical perceptions trigger any type of inquiry into whether "smart contract" is actually representative of any particular capability or consequence of blockchain technology? For this to occur, we may need a different initial perception where smart contract (or contract) is itself a distinct topic of blockchain. So perhaps a more appropriate inquiry would be to probe if smart contract is indeed a topic of blockchain technology. But it is unclear if such an inquiry will trigger from the initial perceptions created by the term – smart contracts.

Perhaps, smart contract could be an example of a colloquial term that's best left out of blockchain terminology. In addition to misrepresenting blockchain's capabilities and consequences, it can cause distractions into non-existent adjacent subject matters (e.g., artificial intelligence). At the same time, validating the initial skepticism could result in learning the topic of blockchain contracts. So, maybe smart contract does not belong in the foundational terminology of blockchain but is a good candidate for the reinforcing terminology.

On its own, there is nothing unfamiliar about this term. Familiarity generally results in analogies. Will this term create analogous perceptions of blockchain technology with other subsystems for recording transactions like a DBMS? So, the real question is, can this term create an appropriate initial perception that can lead to an understanding of <u>how</u> blockchain technology is a subsystem for recording transaction and yet unlike other similar subsystems? For although this designer term is representative of blockchain capabilities, it can cause some misconceptions if (wrong) analogies become part of the learning process.

Likely initial perceptions:

Complete familiarity can also be misleading if it distracts us from finding any similarities and differences between the actual subject matter and the analogies. The most likely analogous initial perception will be about blockchain being potentially similar to a DBMS. As such, perception of DBMS can mix into the perception of blockchain. So it is important that these initial perceptions triggers inquiries that probe into the differences between blockchain and DBMS (and any other analogies of subsystems for recording transactions).

It is important to note that analogies are useful in learning so long as it's not misused as a replacement for actual understanding of the subject matter. Also, it is not clear as to how many analogies and analogous perceptions would be needed to complete the learning. In the case of this particular term, are there additional subsystems of recording transactions (other than DBMS) that should be considered?

Likely inquiries triggered by initial perceptions:

Two types of inquiries are likely to occur – 1) an inquiry to validate the perception of similarities between the subject matter (blockchain) and the analogy (DBMS). 2) An inquiry to validate the perception of differences between the subject matter (blockchain) and the analogy (DBMS).

We may need additional inquiries in scenarios where the term is representative of the subject matter but the analogous perception is incorrect (meaning the analogy is incorrect). For example if the analogy of DBMS is incorrect in context of blockchain technology, then how can we validate an initial analogous perception about DBMS?

So the first inquiry should be if the analogy (DBMS) is correct or incorrect relative to the subject matter (blockchain) followed by the similarities and differences between the analogy and the subject matter. This means that having complete familiarity of a technical term may sound good but there is much more learning necessary before a complete and correct understanding of the subject matter is achieved.

This designer term is an example of a representative term that is completely familiar and as a result will cause initial analogous perceptions. Some analogies can cause misconceptions (hide differences between the subject matter and the analogy). Therefore even if there is complete familiarity, there is a need for deeper inquiry into validating each analogous perceptions.

This designer term is representative of blockchain technologies capabilities and consequences in a big way because it represents the technical core. In fact, this term is an example of a mega-term. Mega-terms represent big parts of a subject matter and tend to be a mixture of familiar and unfamiliar meanings. In this particular case, there is more familiarity with the "decentralized generation" part of the term and there is some unfamiliarity with the "immutable data chains" part of the term.

As a result, the initial perceptions are also likely to be more than one. Some perceptions arising from the familiar parts and other perceptions arising from the unfamiliar parts. From a self-learning point of view, it is important that proper learning from mega-terms occurs. For e.g. any misunderstanding from the term "smart contracts" is less tragic compared with misunderstandings from mega-terms like "decentralized generation of immutable data chains".

Likely initial perceptions:

It is more than likely that there will be multiple perceptions created by the term. At least one perception will emerge from the "decentralized generation" part of the term. The perception will be about a mechanism that is decentralized and capable of generating (creating) an unfamiliar or intriguing result. The second part of the term will give rise to perceptions of specific characteristics that define unchangeable data linked together.

These two perceptions may form independently but are connected to one another. So a correct inquiry would including validating the two perceptions independently, validating the connection between the two perceptions, and validating the two perceptions as a connected whole.

Likely inquiries triggered by initial perceptions:

It is important that the initial perceptions trigger inquiries into the individual parts and the whole (sum of parts). The most likely inquiries would be about the mechanism of decentralized generation, probing the characteristics of immutable data chains and finally inquiring about the consequences of applying the mechanism (decentralized generation) to achieve the characteristic results (immutable data chains).

If these multiple inquiries into blockchain subject matter are partial (not complete), then the learning will be ineffective and the resulting understanding could be meaningless. There must be a coordination of these multiple inquiries to ensure that the learning is properly ordered and builds upon previous understandings.

It is very likely that mega-terms (representative of big parts or pieces of a subject matter) can create multiple intriguing perceptions. This designer term is an example of a mega-term for blockchain technology. As such it could be highly effective as part of the foundational terminology. However, the learning will be complex, requiring multiple validations of the individual perceptions and then a separate validation of the connected perceptions as a whole. If this is not possible, then the mega-term will be inefficient from a self-learning perspective.

As a subject matter, blockchain technology has some aspects that are counter intuitive. This particular technical term may acquaint us with one of those aspects. Blockchain is a system of record for transactions, which is typical. However, the atypical aspect is the subsequent replication of the entire system of record (blockchain) across the entire blockchain network.

Likely initial perceptions:

Systems of record is a familiar technical term and as such the likely initial perception it triggers won't be anything out of the ordinary. It is the connection of this term with replication that will cause a conflicting initial perception. Replication and its variations (duplication, cloning, etc...) is not readily acceptable as a technical best practice. There is a technical and financial cost associated with replication in general. However, replication is one of the foundational aspects of blockchain technology. So, this counter intuitive initial perception is appropriate as it will lead to probing the relevance and consequences of replicating a system of record in blockchain technology.

The conventional view of systems of record could be part of the initial perceptions too. If this familiarity is transferred to blockchain technology, then the initial perception could prove wrong. Because conventionally, there is no replication of a system of record.

Likely inquiries triggered by initial perceptions:

Since the initial perception is likely to include conflicts and counter intuitive to established patterns, the inquiries are likely to be centered on probing the conflicting aspect of replicating a system of record. Questions like, why is replication an essential aspect and what are the consequences of replicating a system of record will be the obvious inquiries.

Conventionally, systems of record are centralized and access to information is controlled through a set of managed access points. Inquiries into whether this conventional view is preserved or even applicable is very important. Another type of inquiry that is very likely would be about alternatives to replication (if any) or ways to mitigate the consequences of replication.

However, there is a possibility that the term system of record is unfamiliar in which case the inquiry is likely to focus on probing on an adjacent subject matter (systems of record). This will be a distraction from the primary subject matter (blockchain) and will make the learning process less efficient. So, even with designer terms that are supposed to provide a direct learning path, the possibility of distraction caused by unfamiliar, adjacent subject matters exists.

As a designer term, replicated system of record is useful in driving home the counter intuitive aspects of blockchain technology. The initial perceptions will cause conflict between the bad practice (replication) and best practice (system of record), leading to a learning path where a deeper probe into the reasons for replication and understanding the consequences of replication becomes a priority.

Tentative conclusions

The case study is useful in forming some tentative conclusions about the definition of a semantically complete terminology and its significance to self-learning. One of the obvious conclusions is that regardless of a terms origin (colloquial or designer), its effect on efficient self-learning is not certain. So the foundational terminology for a specific subject matter and its topics would most likely be a mixture of colloquial and designer terms.

Another important conclusion is that familiarity with terms can be helpful or misleading. Hence, familiar terms should also trigger rigorous inquiries and probing into the subject matter. This is to ensure we learn any specific differences embedded and hidden in the subject matter.

We need to continuously assess and select terms that can support efficient self-learning. This is an important conclusion because terminology evolves and changes. Some terms "stick" and others "drop off" over time. However, if we are to ensure consistent and efficient self-learning that we should ensure the terminology has the right concoction of terms in it.

There are also terms that have zero representation of the associated subject matter (e.g. smart contracts). It may be better to keep these types of terms out of any terminology. These conclusions are not to be trusted until a proper hypothesis, experiment(s), and theory is established to understand semantically complete terminologies and their effect on efficient self-learning. However, the tentative conclusions are useful in guiding further research on this topic and even extending the research to include self-learning by machines.

Today, machines learn by applying specialized algorithms to very high volumes of diverse data. This learning happens without the capability or use of perceptions. Perceptions only come into play when machines leverage additional input from humans as part of its learning process. This is when human perceptions become part of machine learning, indirectly for machines and unknowingly to humans.

Let's assume that at some point humans and machines will not only learn on their own (unsupervised) but will also learn or confirm their self-learning by sharing their respective knowledge. In this scenario, a common terminology would make learning and subsequent confirmed learning more efficient. The challenges are many including the absence of a common language and vocabulary between humans and machines.

The blockchain case study is indicative of how unsupervised learning of an emerging (new) subject matter is dependent on appropriate terminology. There is still time to establish semantically complete terminologies, particularly for subjects and topics where human and machine learning is likely to converge.

Summary

Humans have several avenues for learning and understanding a subject matter at different levels of scope and detail. Training (supervised learning), self-study (unsupervised learning) and experimentation (trial and error) are some of the different ways to learn. All these avenues are based on using a terminology to represent and elaborate the individual topics of a subject matter.

This paper highlights the significance of terms in the formation of initial perceptions and the importance of these perceptions in how quickly we establish the correct understanding of a subject matter. The longer the initial perception stays in our mind, the harder it is to overcome. "Sticky" initial perceptions could become a big hurdle for the learning process. It should be our objective that through learning we validate or invalidate the initial perceptions and when necessary replace it with reasoned, mature, knowledgeable perceptions.

If we don't care about a particular subject matter, then any knowledge or understanding of that subject matter sounds meaningless. If we do care about a subject matter, even for short period, then it is important to acquire the right knowledge and understanding as efficiently as possible. This makes the learning process significant and anything that can accelerate our holistic understanding of the subject matter becomes very important.

This paper outlines a tentative model for looking into the role of terminology in (self) learning a subject matter. In this context, we start with the hypothesis that a semantically complete terminology of a subject matter is an asset for efficient self-learning. The model progresses from a broad hypothesis to a narrower approach for defining and determining semantic completeness of terms. A series of steps guides the progression – from an overview of the role of a terminology in learning a subject matter, to a definition of semantically complete terminology of technical subject matter, and finally to using the blockchain technology subject matter as a case study for assessing the quality of individual terms.

There could be several, constructive outcomes of assessing the quality of a terminology. We could get foundational and reinforcing terminologies for a subject matter. We could also determine any negative effects of colloquial terms and have the option of replacing such terms with new designer terms. As a result, we can maintain the semantic completeness of terminologies on an ongoing basis.

The idea of semantically complete terminology for subject matters will become exponentially more significant if it becomes useful in machine learning. If we can imagine that semantically complete terminologies can become useful in driving self-learning for humans and machines alike, then we get closer to the outcome of establishing a common understanding of a subject matter.

The tentative models outlined in this paper are just some initial, personal thoughts with no real roots in any particular theory or with any support from empirical evidence. So, a responsible next step would be to dive deeper into the notion of semantically complete terminologies and assess if there is any credence to it. Most likely, we have only scratched the surface of this subject matter.

A heat map of the subject matter will reveal that there is much to explore before the tentative model can become a robust model capable of launching credible research into semantic completeness of terminologies. For this, deeper expertize in human learning, semantics, and terminologies is necessary.

Boundaries for exploring semantic completeness of terminologies

Role of terminologies in self-learning a subject matter

Semantic completeness of non-technical terminologies

Definition of a semantically complete terminology for technical subject matters

Other avenues for learning a subject matter

Quality of semantically complete terminologies for machine learning and human (self) learning

Assessing the quality of a semantically complete terminology for blockchain technology

We also need to tie the right type of empirical evidence to the tentative model. Without that the underlying assumptions like "our initial perceptions trigger learning" will remain logically weak. Can we be definitive whether it's better to not use any semantically incomplete terms or its worth taking on the risk of misleading perceptions resulting from incomplete and inaccurate terms?

In the case study, we did not assess the reinforcing terminology for blockchain (terms like "blockchain is not a database"). This may not be important to the final outcome of creating specialized terminologies for enabling self-learning. We may not ascertain if this is an acceptable logic unless we have a complete case study of foundational and reinforcing terminologies.

The brief and high-level exploration of colloquial and designer terms in blockchain terminology gave us some insights into the diverse set of likely initial perceptions. These perceptions had skepticism, intrigue, counter intuitive aspects, or complete familiarity leading to underestimation and misconceptions. Knowing which term is likely to create what type of perceptions and inquiries can be a step in ensuring only the right terms exist in our terminologies for self-learning.

Future versions of this paper will capture and outline a more conclusive model for determining the significance of semantically complete terminologies in self-learning.

References

1. Technical terms, http://www.mit.edu/course/21/21.guide/techterm.htm
2. Understanding semantic analysis (and why this title is totally Meta), https://zetaglobal.com/blog-posts/understanding-semantic-analysis-title-totally-meta/
3. Discourse semantics with information structure, https://academic.oup.com/jos/search-results?fl_SiteID=5212&SearchSourceType=1&access_openaccess=true
4. Introduction to the research topic meaning in mind: semantic richness effects in language processing, https://www.frontiersin.org/articles/10.3389/fnhum.2013.00723/full